A Letter to a Friend

(Thoughts on Living as a Gay Man)

What They're Saying About 'A Letter to a Friend'

This is really so touching for me and I am sure for a lot of other gay men who are out and who want to be out... I just have to say thank you for this; it is very inspirational.

~*Kelvin*

Insightful, helpful, thought provoking and so very worth reading… more than once. Thanks for sharing this. Thirteen years later and there are still so many that need to read this letter as they struggle with their decision to live or not to live. Thank you, Doug, for freely and consistently sharing with us. As I was reading it I did realize that this is definitely for gay and non-gay people as confusion is truly nondiscriminatory!

1 ♥

~*Shari-Lynn*

Powerful!

~*Kenneth*

Best letter ever written to a true friend. It's amazing and beautiful

~Michael J

Thank you for sharing this heartfelt and sensible letter with us. Every SGL (Same-Gender Loving) person should read this. Very inspiring!

~O. Morisset

This is one of the most amazing letters I have ever read to say the least. It is so wonderfully put. I needed to read this today. Reading this has changed me today... to being more hopeful of tomorrow... less hurt about people's views of my life, ... and more connected to God's love. That is due to everyone. Thank you for sharing this!!

~Bridget

BEAUTIFUL.

~Tyranus

Thanks Doug for such a heart-to-heart message. Your letter to Greg was also a letter to Anthony!

~Anthony W.

Very Powerful!

~Maurice

… this is FIRE.....LOVE it...

~T. Hayes

Truly inspirational.

~Brian

Doug, I used 'A Letter to a Friend' in a class I facilitate for young guys struggling with their sexual identity.

~R. Scott

Beautifully, beautifully written Doug. Thank you for sharing such an intimate and heartfelt letter

~Kay W.

OMG...simply amazing. Speechless. I wish someone would have had this dialog with me many years ago when I was so confused and conflicted. I love this, Doug Cooper- Spencer!

~Daryl

Absolutely beautiful! Thank you for sharing something so intimate. It touched me and I'm sure many others. You put into beautiful, vivid words something I experience daily which is simply existing happily as an out, queer being on a spiritual journey. Thank you again!

~*R. M.*

I love how beautiful and honest the truth is.

~*Tyrus*

This is amazing, Doug. Inspired. Your heart must've been overflowing the moment you put pen to paper. And, Greg, what a gift this must've been for you. You're a very fortunate man. You two are fortunate to have found each other.

~*Allen*

WOW! Doug, this is truly beautiful, honest, real and TRUE. I'm moved beyond actual words. ((TRULY BEAUTIFUL)) and what makes it even more moving is the fact that ten- plus years down the line, the two of you are still together, LOVE IS TRULY BEAUTIFUL. I see you mentioned it in an early post but would you be okay with me sharing this with some of my friends? Things here in Kenya are reminiscent of 1972 US and even though it might not eliminate all forms of homophobia, it will go a long way in making visualizing a better tomorrow possible. Hope you are okay with that. Guys need to know there really is a ray of light at the end of the tunnel and this letter goes a long way demonstrating just that. Thanks for sharing and I hope those that I share this with will be able to have a more positive outlook towards the challenges family, society and life throw their way. Thank you. ☺

~*Fiona, Kenya*

***What they're saying about 'This Place of Men',
'People Like Us' and 'Leaving Gomorrah'***

… an amazing piece of work. The story is interesting
and well told… kept my interest… kept me guessing.
(The) writing is clear and crisp, the words are well
chosen, and the prose is often beautiful and
evocative... Doug Cooper-Spencer has a natural gift
as a storyteller.

> *~ Keith Boykin, former White House Advisor,
Clinton Administration; CNBC News contributor;
CNN Commentator; host of BET J's 'My Two Cents';
Editor, The Daily Voice; author "One More River to
Cross", "Respecting the Soul", "Beyond the
Downlow"; Editor of 'For Colored Boys Who Have
Considered Suicide When the Rainbow Is Still Not
Enough: Coming of Age, Coming Out, and Coming
Home"*

"One of the best books I have ever read about being a
black, gay man…"

> *~ Demetrius Bady, writer for TV series
'Single Ladies'; writer, director for TV
series 'Moesha'.*

This Place of Men offers an interesting example of conflict resolution… There's a side story… which will probably surprise most readers. This Place of Men is a bittersweet love story and Doug Cooper-Spencer has a mature, seasoned voice. It will probably be enjoyable to readers who tire of the usual "we're gay and fabulous" storylines.

~Rod McCullom, 'Rod 2.0' website;
journalist CNN, The Advocate

This Place of Men is the great work of fiction that I wished I had read during my most heightened struggles with sexuality. Cooper-Spencer brilliantly details the two men on a journey to self-love, but in a culture where especially black men are encouraged to wear masks of caricature, denial, and self-hate. The writing in this novel captures the precise and deliberate care of an author who goes beyond troupes of deferred dreams and prodigal sons to paint a vivid picture of men who must get beyond their fear of not being loved in order to embrace love. "This Place of Men" is my Brokeback Mountain. It is the poetic portrait of the healing that can happen when men find the courage to love themselves just the way God created them."

~Tim'm T. West, author "Red Dirt
Revival", "BARE", and "Flirting"

I finished reading the entire This Place of Men Trilogy, and must say I was sad to come to the end of the last book in the trilogy, 'Leaving Gomorrah' because the world I had come to share with Otis, Terrell, Antonio and the many wonderful characters that peopled the trilogy was one of intimacy; so intimate, in fact that I didn't want to leave them behind. BRAVO for the This Place of Men Trilogy!

~Yvonne T.

I loved your book!!! I'll be reading it a second time… Again, savoring every minute. The book and it's people really lived for me. I didn't want to leave that world behind… I applaud your graceful use of language, the deft pacing and the honest ease of it. It felt authentic... Thank You for *This Place of Men*
~(Allen, Chicago IL)

We're eagerly awaiting the next installment
~(Bongani Bingwa, South Africa)

Read both books and now I can't wait to read the 3rd in the trilogy. Awesome, awesome work!
~ Kanuri Keevon Young, New York City

"This book is so beautifully written. So mesmerizing, enchanting. 'People Like Us' is my favorite in the trilogy"

~Mc Makhalima, South Africa

I started reading 'This Place of Men' and I already know I want to read the whole trilogy. You had me at the first page.

~ P. Schultz, Bremen, Germany

Amazon Reviews:

Extremely good reading… interesting twists… Thanks for your eye opener!

A great story and a core truth: The life you've been prepared for isn't the one meant for you; sometimes it's not even the life you've been given… The book doesn't beat you over the head with that truth, but the writer puts it together artfully… you find yourself understanding it even though it's never plainly stated…. the mark of a good story and a good writer.

Awesome book! This Place of Men is an awesome story. Doug Cooper-Spencer proves that he is as great a writer as his contemporaries… the characters in this book are most captivating and the story pulses to an unexpected climax. My only disappointment is that I have to wait for another Cooper-Spencer book.

Saw this book a few weeks ago… picked it up as the back cover caught my interest and I am so glad I did… I fell in love with this book as it is many wondrous things: love story, the Black family, and a story that (makes) one think… The characters are well written, some surprises, and again a wonderful read… I've never heard of the author and I feel that I know my Black Gay authors, but this one snuck under my radar.

(This Place of Men) has very good views on problems that exist in the gay community… This Place of Men is asking us to identify the place that we have in our community by confronting the reality of our sexual identity and make a stand for these principles.

~Amazon Reviews

Also by Doug Cooper-Spencer:

'This Place of Men' (novel)

'People Like Us' (novel)

'Leaving Gomorrah' (novel)

'The Wounded Gardener' (short story)

'A Question of Commitment' (short story)

'Bad Damon' (short story)

'The Summer of '63' (short memoir)

'The Visitation 1964' (short memoir)

"Growing up gay is a challenge. In a hostile world that refuses to validate your existence, being same-gender loving or even transgender quite often requires giving up modes of self-validation and refuting self-worth. From the day you first realize your difference, you immediately draw strategies of defense. Those measures can range anywhere from outright confrontation to secrecy and denial. Now, also consider self-love in your strategy." ~ *Doug Cooper Spencer*

Forward

A Letter to a Friend' was written in 1999 by Doug Cooper to his then boyfriend, Gregory Spencer, a year into their relationship. It was during a time when Gregory, having just come out to his family, was being pressured by some family members to 'reconsider' his decision to live as a gay man.

What began as a personal letter to Gregory eventually became a manifesto against homophobia and a declaration of liberation from homophobia. Giving thought to homophobic tropes and devices such as the idea of God's condemnation of homosexuality, and the view that declares homosexuality as unnatural, 'A Letter to a Friend' challenges those worn ways of thinking with fresh ideas.

'A Letter to a Friend' offers words and thoughts for anyone who wants to break the bonds of homophobia, be they same-gender loving, or those who simply are brave enough to take a fresh look at old ideas. 'A Letter to a Friend' implores all of us to take another look at ways of thinking that have held many captive to oppression and bigotry and to move to a spirit that seeks to realize a self-actualized spirit anchored in love.

Doug and Gregory Cooper-Spencer have now been together for fourteen years since they first met in 1998.

A Letter to a Friend

(Thoughts on Living as a Gay Man)

November 14, 1999

Dear Greg,

I hope this letter finds you well, or at least in a better place than when we last talked. I know I promised not to bother you for the next (what, few weeks? Months? You never really said) while you decided whether or not you wanted to live your life as a gay man. Believe me, I want you to make that decision because it's the life you will have to live. But I want to give you some things to think about while you make your decision. They are thoughts about being gay that most people don't understand or don't want to. They are points that I hope will make things clearer to you about who you are as a gay man.

You said your family is unhappy now that they know you're gay. You said they refuse to believe it and that you're simply going through a phase that's being helped along by bad influences. Believe me, their response is quite usual. Just like so many others, they say they have your best interest at heart—and this might be true, though sometimes it's their own self-interest that's at stake. Still, quite often their ignorance gets in the way of their understanding, and it's ignorance that has been passed down from old ways of thinking. It's their misunderstanding that results in their disdain of your sexual orientation.

While they might not understand being gay, it should be your duty to understand because it's your life. The life you have been given.

Greg, this letter is from my heart to you because of the love I have for you. And whatever decision you make I want to know that you made it with a clear mind and with understanding. It's the best I can offer you at this time, and I hope you appreciate what I'm about to tell you. Well, here goes:

Your Homosexuality is Merely a Difference

~Let me start off by saying that homosexuality is no more exclusive than differences in height or weight; from those who might have a natural tendency towards obesity compared to some who for the life of them can't gain weight at all. It's no different than those who are born to function primarily with their left hand while others who are born without hands at all; or those who have near incomparable physical strength and those whose frailty allowed them to live only for a day.

In nature's tendency towards diversity we've been given people whose minds mainly grasp abstractions while others, logic. It's the will of the force of nature that deals in diversity—just look around at the different races and characteristics on this planet. If nature can offer such diversity, why then would homosexuality not be part of that diversity? Your homosexuality is not so much an aberration as merely a difference, a variation that compliments the natural diversity of life.

The Cause of Social Trauma

~There will be some who will tell you the fact that you might choose to live your life as an openly gay person would only cause pain to your loved ones. Don't believe them. As someone who has been out for a long time (even before you were born *smile*) I can tell you that all of your loved ones won't be against you. Nonetheless, your sexuality will not be the cause of pain for those who might claim 'to suffer'. It's not your sexuality that's causing their pain, but ignorance, fear and their own bias that's causing them pain. It's the same ignorance that at one time made society turn its back on the physically challenged, or those today who claim their problems on 'the others'.

Sadly, it's never the pain brought on by the detractors' own social or personal maladies that's investigated. Instead they choose to make others the source of their discomfort. Quite often people will form fragile matrixes in which to house their own shortcomings.

Oh, and please Do Not let your detractors get away with trying to lump you into the category of rapists and molesters. Rapists and molesters harm. Heterosexual and homosexual rapists and molesters cause harm. Heterosexuality and homosexuality in and of themselves does not cause harm.

Nature's Way?

~Some people say homosexuality is unnatural. I don't believe this and I hope you come to agree. Your homosexual orientation developed as a course of nature, it was not artificially induced. Therefore it's natural (just as it is in many other species of animals). Quite often what is meant by those who use the terms 'unnatural' or 'not normal' is that your sexual orientation doesn't match that person's moral beliefs; the same term was used decades ago in matters of interracial marriage.

That stated, understand that the implications of such an argument goes further than it appears. It underscores the reasoning that homosexuality is a matter of choice (in that case, why not heterosexuality as well). It's the implication that since it's a choice and not of nature, it's not of God; therefore it can be (and should be) undone.

Look, only you know the depth and history of your feelings, only you know if you 'chose' your sexual orientation- - of course I know you didn't, just as your 'straight' siblings didn't choose theirs. However, only you know this and you do not owe anyone else an explanation unless you choose to do so. Given the pain and the disenfranchisement that many LGBT persons go through in life, I doubt many would have 'chosen' their sexuality.

And let's not forget the 'anatomical fit' argument. Some will call attention to 'incorrect' anatomical fit as an argument to support their claim of the unnaturalness of homosexuality. This claim is ridiculous. To use that argument clearly shows ignorance towards an understanding of sexual orientation. A person's sexual orientation, whether homosexual or heterosexual, is how a person feels and perceives sexually. It doesn't clearly define the types of sexual acts a person will engage in. A celibate heterosexual is still heterosexual because of the way he or she sexually feels and perceives more than the sexual act the person engages in.

Also, to use such an argument of anatomical correctness would preclude any sexual act aside from penis to vagina. While some might say 'yes' to this, it's clearly not human to live that way. There are other sexual acts that heterosexuals perform that are 'anatomically incorrect' as well. Let's see how many of them will stop engaging in oral sex! Besides, other than reasons of public health or a clear violation of another's wish for life and safety, why should society come into anyone's bedroom anyway?

All of these arguments can get so crazy. However, I want you to remember to love yourself just as you love the skin you're in. It's the gift God gave you. It called Life. Yours.

God and Morality

~Let's start with morality, first. The matter of morality will often come up when people discuss gay lifestyle. Here's something I hope you will remember: We think of morality as inflexible codes of conduct. But in fact our values and our moral precepts are not so inflexible. They can be very pliant. History has shown us that. For instance, the difference between the moral standards that once held the idea of women as an adjunct to men, or ones that supported the belief of the inferiority of black people to whites are vastly different than moral standards of today.

Morality can be used to protect and enlighten in the most divine way, or it can be actualized as an agent of great harm and destruction. Only accept those things in life that do not harm others or yourself and things that nurture and create a positive energy for both you and your environment. So unless it can truly be proven that being gay works against this positive force, feel free to embrace it with the warmth your beliefs and your values deserve no matter what others might think.

~Now, of course the subject of morality always leads to conversation about God. It's a touchy subject, but this is what I'd like to propose: God is an abstract concept that humankind has honed to explain phenomena such as being, death and circumstance, inexplicable matters that govern life. There are many views, all of which claim divine providence.

To say the concept of God is an abstraction is not to suggest that God doesn't exist. I, for one believe God does exist in some form or another. It's just that our ability to fully understand this power we term 'God' is greatly lacking. It's very difficult to understand something that can't be fully realized as fact.

Even to the point that we have come to apply anthropomorphic terms to describe God speaks of our desire to explain It. In the end, we can only come to terms with It, not explain It. We can't explain or understand something so powerful, so infinite as the energy we have chosen to call God.

Beyond it all, this is where faith comes into play. So many people profess faith when all they really have is belief. Someone once described belief as wishing things to be as you are told they should be, and faith as a letting go of expectation, to be able to throw your arms open and accept what is not known or understood. Our beliefs are shaped by cultural, political and to some degree, personal influence, but very little faith. Personally, I can say that belief taught me fear, but now, my faith informs me of love.

Finally, regarding God, I can't leave this subject without addressing the idea that God does not condone homosexuality. Using our concept of God, I challenge such a notion to be proven. If God is omniscient, then It knows who is going to be gay.

Of course, such a reply will almost always lead to a discussion about Free Will—the belief that through the grace of God, we are given a chance to make choices in life. Such reasoning falls short in its rationalization. To accept the idea of free will as an explanation of my homosexuality would be akin to accepting the argument of 'choice'. Even the idea of free will as grace from God is arguable if it's set within the context of retribution. If God punishes us for our choices then free will was not given out of grace. I do not believe a divine entity that possesses omnipotence has need for free will. It would simply control what we do, not allowing us to fail, and therefore would have no need to resort to retribution.

We have no idea of the wonder of 'The Mystery' we have chosen to call God. 'The Mystery' simply Is. How much control we have in divining our lives is small compared to the greatness of The Mystery.

The Mystery, God, created me to be in this life at this time and I will love Its wisdom without question because I know I live a life that has far more love and meaning than what some have tried to deny me. In that I take solace.

Speaking of God and spirituality, while you and I have talked about it on many occasions, let me warn you that people will attempt to use their religious beliefs to sway you to see things their way. I know because just like everyone else, I've been subjected to such, and here's what I've decided: I've come to refuse beliefs that are borne of culture and politic. I choose a faith that liberates me from such precepts and simply embraces the idea that everyone has the right to become self actualized towards a spirit that causes no harm to self or others, a nurturing spirit. Therefore, I choose to walk a spiritual path (stumbling sometimes as humans do), than a religious one. The two are not the same because religion is man-made and is prone to all the influences I stated above, while spirituality is the essence of God. Many seek religion (earthly power), but few seek spirituality.

This is what I've come to use to shape my spiritual view. Use it if you choose to do so.

Love

~Greg, you are a very kind and loving person. I know that. So don't let anyone convince you that because you're gay, you are less than that: A kind and loving person. And let that carry you like a vessel to kind and loving people and to kind and loving experiences.

People define love in so many ways; some are on the mark, while others, I think, miss it completely. The best definition of love I've ever read is by M. Scott Peck. He defines love to be "The will to extend one's self for the purpose of nurturing one's own or another's spiritual growth." I choose to love myself in this way and seek this kind of love from others. I will demand it so I might know it. I have all the right in the world to seek the nurturance of my spirit free from the whims of others. I reject the games people play in their attempt to gain dominance over my life; it's been done to many throughout the ages.

I understand that when you learn to love yourself, you're able to love others and you grow beyond the borders of religious doctrine and demagoguery towards a true spiritual journey. You become open to wondrous things about your life, about Life period. You become the person God meant you to be.

In the end, I accept that the brilliance of 'The Mystery' we call God and Life will probably always continue, and will probably never be understood. And that 'The Mystery' is not as frightening as it might sound. It is fear that holds most of us captive to lives of trepidation, hatred and inconsequence while love sets us free.

Procreation

~By now I'm sure you've heard time and again that homosexuality is contagious and could bring about the end of procreation. When I first heard this as a young man I was horrified because I felt like I was taking part in ending life as we know it. But I was so much younger then!

Life is much more of a force than we might want to consider. I don't believe if those of us who are homosexual act on our nature, then everyone will become homosexual and procreation would cease. Everyone would not become homosexual if someone who is homosexual chooses to live his or her life. Humans are not that monolithic.

Besides, if procreation is the prime reason for the validation of our existence, then we are all in step to miss the fullness that makes us human. I believe the positive growth of our individual spirit (one imbued in love) is the prime agent of our individual lives, not the extension of the physical self. And anyway, given our tenuous relationship with the ecosystem, adoption would be a suitable fit.

The propagation of life is a powerful force. We do not know that sexual intercourse is exclusively needed to procreate. All living beings don't engage in sexual intercourse in order to procreate (asexual reproduction). Therefore, we shouldn't assume humans, if given the fate of the cessation of intercourse would no longer generate offspring. It might sound strange, but it is biologically plausible. Life and the reproduction of life have proven to be just that powerful.

Family

~ Given what you've told me about your family, they aren't any different from other families. They are a solid unit. This is good. However, be prepared to have people tell you that homosexuality causes the destruction of the family. This doesn't have to be true. If a family is firmly entrenched in love it will not allow the fact that one of its members is gay destroy it. If it does, then it needs to re-evaluate its shortcomings because matters of diversity as well as adversity will always arise within the family structure. That is the challenge of love. That is the challenge of family.

Life After Coming Out

~Right now it might seem to you that there can be no future living as a gay person. But that's because you have little to go by in referencing living as an affirming gay man. Over the past year we've been together, though you've been hesitant to see the community you can be a part of, I want you to know that it is a great community full of the diversity, adversity, joy and pain that any community can have. And it's large! No, HUGE! It's a community that reaches every part of the world and one that has existed in one form or another since the existence of human kind.

Aside from the boy-hood dating and sex of your adolescence you've told me about, all you've seen of gay life has been just that: secret sex and adolescent romance. But there is so much more. Believe me.

You've seen my life and you know that I am living it just as well as any other person, with just as much joy and pain as anyone would encounter in life. And this, coming from someone who had to go through so much more than you have to go through today, having come out when I did.

1972 was not the greatest year to come out. There were strict laws against gay people. Arrests. Brutality against us that went without punishment. Housing and job discrimination (I personally have been denied housing and was also kicked out of the military, but one day I believe even that will change). It was horrible. But I, like so many, made it through, stumbling and getting back up many, many times. The journey wasn't without merit, though. It wasn't without merit because with each whack of the stick, each smash of the fist, each door closed in the face and each act of rejection the way was paved for the equality that is finally coming.

You have a community that can offer you great friends and experiences the world over. It's a community that does have many, many straight allies who will embrace you for who you are. But more than anything, it's a community that can show you that life goes on in a wondrous way. Please believe that.

Part II

The Lessons
(Short Essays)

~~~~

FEAR AND FAITH

People will try to instill fear in you to intercept your journey to finding and accepting your identity as a gay man. They will use many tactics, but the most often used weapons are God, abandonment, disenfranchisement, and sometimes, even violence. They use these weapons because they are choice weapons to instill fear. But let me tell you about a weapon you can use to conquer any fear that might arise: faith.

Fear and faith. How do we come by both and how do we use them?

On the surface we would see the two, faith and fear, as being polar opposites; one (faith) engenders 'fearlessness' while the other feeds into feelings of hopelessness and despair. But in fact both of these energies are firmly rooted in one's sense of self worth.

Of the two energies, fear is the more immediate and, as a result is more tenable. That's why it's used so often as a way to control others. It's a primal response that's wired into every animal and can switch on at the drop of a dime.

Now, fear isn't a bad thing since it serves to both protect us from real harm as well as regulate our actions. Without it, we would all just march into the jaws of a lion or commit heinous acts without knowledge of reprisal. However, if left unchecked fear can run rampant and cause the very harm it's supposed to protect us from.

Faith, on the other hand, is more complex because it isn't hotwired into our primal responses. We have to work for it. We have to make a conscious effort to reach into a higher part of ourselves and grope around for something that is not as immediately tenable as fear. However, the result is well worth the labor.

How do we get past fear to a point of faith? I believe it's best to take on the object of your fear in incremental steps and with great understanding. Taking small steps allows time to meditate on the object of your fear bit by bit until you can move beyond it. My own struggle to overcome the fear of someone knowing I was gay is an example.

From childhood through my early twenties I hid the fact that I was attracted to the same sex. Finally, the sheer exhaustion from years of hiding took its toll and I was forced to re-evaluate my situation. I came to stop spending so much time despising myself as the creature I had been led to believe I was to understanding *who* I was; you see, I went from a place of fear to a place of understanding. And one of the things I came to understand was that none of the people who held their weapon of fear over my head could tell me much about me. They had not walked a mile in my shoes. So for them to make their assertions became, to me, a point of them being arrogant as well as ignorant, not only of my life but of life in general. But my acceptance of self-love didn't come overnight; it was through those incremental steps that I was able to achieve it.

A point about faith: You cannot have faith if you don't love yourself. That is probably the first step towards acquiring it. You can have hope, but you can't have faith. Knowing yourself, understanding yourself, excusing yourself and loving yourself, all these acts bring about energy and renewal. It opens us up to great potential and faith is but a part of the power gained.

Now, I know loving yourself can sometimes be a challenge when people are telling you otherwise, but what do they know? No one knows all the answers. See this and you will be able to put them and their views in perspective. Stop giving them power by agreeing with them. Only you and God know you, and none of us truly have the capacity to fully comprehend God, so let go of all the bull crap and move on to a place of love.

Someone once said that faith is letting go of expectation, to be able to throw your arms open and accept what is not known or understood. We should always embrace a faith that will bring about good.

~~~~

THE NAME I CALL MYSELF
(A Lesson on Identity)

Once you know who you are, make sure to name who you are. Identify in truth who you are. They are one in the same, and it is important. Some may tell you that naming yourself is little more than labeling yourself. There's been a dialogue going on for years in the black LGBT/SGL community regarding identity. There are many who refuse to call themselves 'gay', 'lesbian', etc., and that's all fine; there's always room for discussion and shifting paradigms. But what I often notice is for many, the discussion tends to center on what not to call ourselves, often falling short of naming ourselves and giving identity to our lives. Instead, what I hear is the argument to not 'label' one's self, when, in reality, the effects of identifying one's self in truth and labeling one's self aren't that analogous.

What is interesting about some of those very people who are black and same-gender loving but who shun naming themselves in truth is that they are ready to embrace other names that identify them as black people, as gender specific (man, woman), but aren't so ready to give identity to their sexual orientation. By calling myself a black man, am I labeling myself or identifying myself? There is a difference.

Labeling can restrict people to description; unlike owning a name, it risks falling short of illuminating the self-worth of the subject. By labeling a person we fail to recognize the fullness of the spirit and the vitality with which the person is imbued. On the other hand, naming yourself-identifying yourself in truth gives voice to who you are; it speaks of your history, your community, your potential and that sense of rightful place. A label becomes a name when you give it life. The differences are subtle, yet substantial.

Are we merely our name? Of course not. We're more. However, in stating we're more we also acknowledge our name as a relative to all the other components that makes us who we are. To do otherwise would be to pigeonhole ourselves. And yeah, that would be foolish.

It would be foolish for me to look no further than the fact that I'm a same-gender- loving man, just as it would be for me to look no further than my blackness, my maleness and other qualities that inform me. Naming myself serves as a resource to connect me, not divide me. Yet I will by no means abdicate any vital part of who I am because each of those qualities determines my thoughts, my values and my actions.

Also, naming yourself is an essential part of loving yourself. You are part of a larger order, but you are also who you are in that larger order and you should be proud of it.

While some may go on talking about what they do not want to be identified as, I hope they remember to also search for an identity that embraces who they truly are, because that will be the essence of who they are (and remember, if it's not truth, then it's not essence). That will be the seed that offers growth.

Greg, just like being black, male, female, daughter, son, brother, sister, cousin or anything else, having an identity refines and empowers personhood. And believe me, since you've already been labeled by people who would oppose your very right to exist, it would be best to name yourself, to own yourself.

~~~~

LOSS AND RENEWAL

Greg, if you do decide to live your life as an openly gay man you should be prepared to lose some things you might consider important. Be prepared to lose some things, but don't worry, because losing things can quite often leave space for new things. With loss comes renewal.

Understand this: we're all afraid of losing things that are important to us. Love, life, money; whatever it is, losing what we've accepted as something valuable to us can be frightening.

For gay men and women, the idea of loss is always near. Losing the love of family and friends, job and respect hangs over our heads with every thought we might have of people finding out about our sexual orientation, so most of the time we simply choose to keep who we really are a secret.

Believe me, Greg, everyone fears loss. But, like anything else, loss deserves understanding, and once it is understood, its effect changes.

What gives the idea of losing things so much power? And how much power should we really give losing something?

On some levels, who we are has been shaped by those elements that have been the most prevalent in our lives. Social constructs, the cultures of family, and tribe are probably the most obvious examples, so to remain associated with those structures gives us a sense of security, even when that sense of security might only offer false hope. Nonetheless, the belief that you're secure becomes comforting.

The need to feel anchored to something is important. That's why we seek that line that keeps us tethered to people, places and things with which we are familiar. That sense of belonging empowers us since as human beings we're social creatures. The idea that we might be without whatever it is that has named us, that has informed us of whom we are and who we are supposed to be can be daunting.

However, while that might be the case, it's important to realize that sometimes we have to shift our attachments or our allegiances; not that we should destroy our relations, but that we have to alter our relations in order to grow. In short, we have to lose something, in order to move on to other things.

Here's an example: When I was in my early twenties, I was a husband (in the traditional sense) and a father, and while I loved my family, I wasn't happy with who I was becoming. My wife wanted the house with the white picket fence in the suburbs and a few more kids. I no longer wanted that. I had begun to grow in different ways and I knew I couldn't live the life she wanted. I had come to terms with the fact that I was gay; I also wanted a life that would lead me to travel the world and explore my creative nature. It was who I felt I was meant to be. But what then? How would I start my life over? And was it right for me to destroy the life I had with my wife and daughter to continue my journey?

Those years were a struggle for me, and they were beginning to take its toll on my sanity, because you see, no one should ever be forced to live imprisoned in a life that's not theirs. Eventually, I had to make that decision to leave the life I had been prepared for in order to lead a new, more unexpected one.

It was painful to leave my wife and my daughter, or so I thought. But then I realized I wasn't leaving them; I was still there. I realized that I was adjusting to a new life that could still include them. Needless to say, the whole scene was ugly when I made the decision to leave my old life; but I knew I was doing what I needed to do to become a more fulfilled person, and also, what my wife and my daughter needed so I could become the best person for them. There were times afterwards when I wondered if I had made the right decision, and after falling on hard times I wondered if I was being punished for my decision. Even some of the people who had once been there for me had turned their backs on me.

But life flows in many directions and along those directions comes different experiences and different people. In time, I came to meet new people who validated me, and with that came new experiences. I can now say I've done what I know I was meant to do with my life. As for my former wife, that choice has helped her as well because she found the life she needed. And my daughter, wow, she has grown into an amazing, independent woman.

In all, I had to lose many things in order to gain wonderful things. Now I know that instead of loss, it was renewal.

Remember, Greg, life moves along many streams. Don't be afraid to put your boat along a different path, because in the end each of those streams flow back to the same ocean.

~~~~~

THE ABSURDITY of DEFENDING YOUR EXISTENCE

People will try to explain why you are gay, as if explaining you will somehow lead to an opening for changing you, or in the least, allow them some resolve as to how they can accept the fact that you exist. *And they will expect you to do the same.* It's an exercise in arrogance, but it will happen nonetheless because humans have the capacity for idealism. To my knowledge we are the only animals that make assumptions as to how we think life *should* be.

If this request, that you explain why you are gay, is asked of you (and it most likely will be asked of you), take it upon yourself to decide whether or not you want to engage in such a discussion. Do not feel obligated, because you aren't.

I've seen this dance play out over the years, where non-gay people will ask gay people to explain their existence and countless gay people over the years who feel they are obligated to entertain heterosexual people with an answer.

I used to ask myself why does this little dance continue to play out, and then it came to me: in conditions of oppression there is a need for the oppressor to lay claim over the oppressed, especially when it comes to determining the nature of, and outcome of those they oppress. This laying of claim often stems from the idea that the oppressed group is not a part of what is acceptable, that they are, in essence, wrong… ruined, and are therefore in need of control by the oppressors. Consequently the oppressed, many having lived a life believing what the oppressors have taught them feel they are obligated to engage their oppressors. It's a crazy mind game in search of authority. The same is true when it comes to this matter of gay people being expected to explain their existence.

Having lived a lifetime of being told they are wrong, many gay people buy into this notion and often feel obligated (believing they are ruined) to appease his or her oppressor. It's a relationship that has been around for a long time, though we are beginning to see, not in all cultures.

As a result of such thinking you will hear explanations from some gay people, or rather defensive statements in an attempt to assuage heterosexuals, to cull some degree of empathy from them over the 'catastrophe' of homosexuality that has befallen the gay person.

You'll hear people rushing to the defense of having been molested to explain they are gay, or that their mother wasn't close to them or that there was no 'strong' male role model in the home, and so on. In all, the discussion revolves around the assumption that the homosexual personality comes from a ruined spirit. But you know what? I don't buy that.

I, for one, do believe I was born to be gay, and I have no trauma as an additional justification, because I have no traumatic situation to hang onto. In a short memoir I wrote called 'The Summer of '63', I recount that summer in 1963 in which I, a nine-year old boy developed a crush on an unsuspecting man. I secretly sought that man every day of that long, hot summer just so I could lay my eyes on him.

Yes, I was a gay child. I was a gay boy without war wounds, plain and simple. No result of trauma. Just gay. I don't know why, just as I don't know why another boy might have liked a woman in his neighborhood. And I'm fine with that unless the concern over my sexuality is part of a larger discussion of life itself. But to single my life out as a person who is gay to have to offer an explanation, I won't play into that demand.

Know this, Greg. No one should feel compelled to explain why he or she exists. No one. By taking the point of view of having to explain one's sexual orientation, we stand to lose out on what it means to empower ourselves, to simply love ourselves for whom we are, cut and dry. No explanations or apologies are needed. That goes for anyone. We should all love ourselves.

And the problem doesn't stop there. By apologizing for being gay we can also potentially hand our power over to the person we're explaining ourselves to. Remember, there are those who don't want to extend unconditional acceptance to a gay lifestyle, and to give people like that an inch, well, they could end up taking a mile.

But you know what, Greg? To say that my existence as a person who is gay has resulted from a traumatic experience brings to mind a great irony, because ironically, the trauma I suffered was from society's demand that I not be who I am. That is a subject that many don't want to touch.

Greg, if you should decide to live as a gay man, and if you find you are asked to explain your existence, it is your choice to do so. But don't feel compelled to answer, because by feeling compelled to answer you hand over authority and only end up belittling yourself.

~~~~~

Closing

Greg, I know growing up gay is a challenge. I've been there and so have many others before you. In a hostile world that refuses to validate your existence, being same-gender loving or even transgender quite often requires giving up modes of self-validation and refuting self-worth. From the day you first realize your difference, you immediately draw strategies of defense. Those measures can range anywhere from outright confrontation to secrecy and denial. Now, also consider self-love in your strategy.

This is why I have written this letter. During the clamor in your life surrounding your coming out, I hope you will find a quiet space to read this letter.

Then take what I've written you and live the life you know will bring you the most happiness and that will allow you to pass your joy on to others.

Forever,

Doug

ABOUT THE AUTHOR

Doug Cooper-Spencer is a novelist, essayist, short fiction writer and lecturer living in Cincinnati. He is the author of three novels: 'This Place of Men', 'People Like Us', and 'Leaving Gomorrah' (books I, II, and III of the 'This Place of Men Series') as well as numerous essays and short stories.

His writings have appeared in anthologies as well as reference books, magazines and online sites including his site: Dougcooperspencer.Com and on his blog: 'The View From Here', as well as at his Facebook page.

In 2006 Doug was nominated by Clik Magazine as one of the 'Elite 25' black gay writers.

Doug's years as an advocate for gay rights (which, ironically, began while serving in the military in the 1970's, and which led to his dismissal) have given him a treasure of history that he often uses in his lectures and commentaries on the subject.

Along with his life-partner of fourteen years, Gregory, Doug also co-produced The Eyes Open Festival and was president of The Eyes Open Festival Organization, a non-profit organization that used the arts in the black SGLT community to educate and inspire all communities to wellness. He also appears in the award winning 1996 documentary, 'All God's Children', a film that looks at the role of black gays and the black church.

Currently, Doug is at work on a screenplay, a collection of short fiction and essays, and a fourth novel.

Contact: Authordougcooperspencer@gmail.com;

www.doug.cooperspencer@facebook.com;

doug.cooperspencer@facebook.com;

www.Dougcooperspencer.com;

www.Dougcooperspencer.Blogspot.com